W9-BWZ-565

Adam Frost

THE AWESOME BOOK OF AWESOMENESS

illustrated by Dan Bramall

BLOOMSBURY
NEW YORK LONDON OXFORD NEW DELHI SYDNEY

Text copyright © 2014 by Adam Frost
Illustrations copyright © 2014 by Dan Bramall
With thanks to Joseph Gwinn
All rights reserved. No part of this book my be reproduced or transmitted in any form
or by any mean, electronic or mechanical, including photocopying, recording, or by any
information storage and retrieval system, without permission in writing from the publisher.

First published in Great Britain in September 2014 by Bloomsbury Publishing Plc
Published in the United States of American in September 2015
by Bloomsbury Children's Books, an imprint of Bloomsbury Publishing, Inc.
www.bloomsbury.com

Bloomsbury is a registered trademark of Bloomsbury Publishing Plc

For information about permission to reproduce selections from this book, write to
Permissions. Bloomsbury Children's Books, 1385 Broadway, New York, New York 10018
Bloomsbury books may be purchased for business or promotional use. For information on
bulk purchases please contact Macmillan Corporate and Premium Sales Department at
specialmarkets@macmillan.com

Library of Congress Cataloging-in-Publication Data
available upon request
ISBN 978-1-61963-793-1 (paperback)

Printed in China by Leo Paper Products, Heshan, Guangdong
2 4 6 8 10 9 7 5 3 1

All papers used by Bloomsbury Publishing, Inc., are natural, recyclable products
made from wood grown in well-managed forests. The manufacturing processes
conform to the environmental regulations of the country of origin.

All figures used in this book are believed to be the latest and most accurate figures at
the point of publication unless the copy states otherwise. Where figures are estimates
or approximations, we have tried to make this clear. A selection of books and websites
we used for our facts can be found on the Sources page at the back of the book.

HARD TO STOMACH

We all swallow bits of hair and fluff every day without even noticing. But some people also chew their own hair, especially when they're bored, with gruesome consequences...

Apple 2.5 inches (in.)

DVD 4.7 in.

Hedgehog 8 in.

Soccer ball 8.7 in.

Largest-ever hair ball
14.8 in. x 7 in. x 7 in.

In November 2007, doctors at Rush University Medical Center in Chicago reported they removed a 10 pound (lb) hair ball from a woman's stomach. It measured 14.8 in. x 7 in. x 7 in.

I'LL EAT ANYTHING

The strangest things ever found in a shark's stomach.

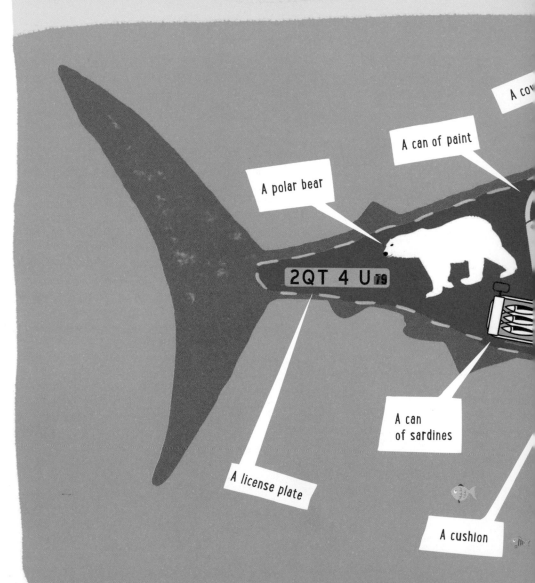

SURF'S UP

How big was the biggest wave ever recorded?

The wave hit Lituya Bay, Alaska, on July 9, 1958.

Biggest-ever wave 1,719 feet (ft)

Whee!

Empire State Building 1,454 ft

Canary Wharf (One Canada Square) 774 ft

Great Pyramid 455 ft

London Eye 443 ft

Big Ben 316 ft

SNOT FUNNY

You swallow about 4 cups
of snot every day.
So how much do you drink...

In a week?

Sink full
of snot

In a month?

Fish tank full
of snot

In 3 months?

Bath full of snot

In a year?

Pool full of snot

FANGS A LOT

If a vampire fed on 1 person every day, and that person also became a vampire, here's what would happen...

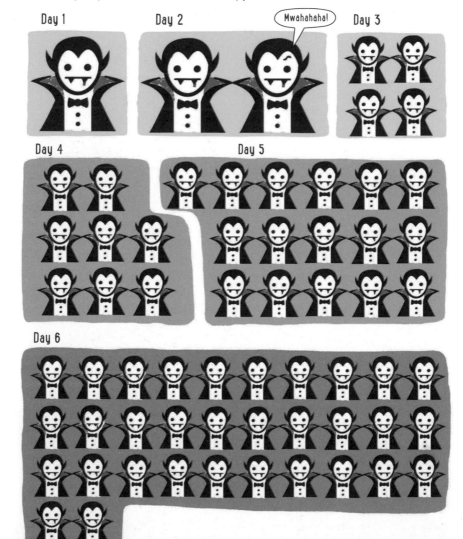

Day 7

Day 8

Day 27

Everyone in Great Britain is a vampire.

Day 34

Everyone in the world is a vampire.

A NEW LEAF

One of the oldest living things on Earth is a nearly 5,000-year-old tree known as Methuselah. So what has happened on the planet since it started growing?

2560 BC
Great Pyramid completed

2832 BC
Methuselah starts to grow

1700 BC
Mammoth becomes extinct

2000 BC
Stonehenge completed

51 BC
Cleopatra becomes Queen of Egypt

79 AD
Vesuvius erupts, burying Pompeii

Nearly 5,000 years later, Methuselah is still here.

1492
Christopher Columbus discovers America

Hello!

1969
Man lands on the moon

A BIT DENSE

In some countries it can get a bit crowded...

Singapore

19,863
people per square mile

Bangladesh

2,678
people per square mile

UK

679

people per square mile

Canada

10

people per square mile

NEED A LIFT?

The average man can lift around 127 pounds (lb) — which is roughly his own body weight. Sounds impressive until you look at how animals measure up.

A dung beetle can pull **1,141** times its own body weight.

That's like **YOU** pulling two fire engines along.

A rhinoceros beetle can lift **850** times its own weight.

That's like **YOU** lifting up three elephants.

A leafcutter ant can lift **50** times
its own body weight with its jaws.

That's like **YOU** picking up
a car with your teeth.

A gorilla can lift **20** times
its own body weight.

That's like **YOU** carrying
two refrigerators.

NEED FOR SPEED

What's the fastest you can go in some different countries (in miles per hour)?

50
Vietnam

50
Iceland

70
UK

80
Poland

85
USA (on one highway in Texas)

ZOOM! ZOOM!

NO LIMIT
Germany (on the Autobahn)

WIND POWER

The loudest burp ever was expelled by
Paul Hunn of the UK in August 2009. Burps
and other noises are measured in decibels.

BLOW-DRYER

70
DECIBELS

ALARM CLOCK

80
DECIBELS

MOTORCYCLE

95
DECIBELS

ELECTRIC DRILL

100
DECIBELS

LAWN MOWER

105 DECIBELS

LOUDEST BURP EVER

109.9
DECIBELS

RAINBOW BLOOD

Living things have different-colored blood. But what color?

Red

Humans and most animals

Octopuses

Crabs/Lobsters

Blue

Green

Samkos bush frog

Sea cucumber

Yellow

Clear

Spiders and some insects

WATER, WATER EVERYWHERE?

Almost three quarters of our planet is water. But how much can we use?

Another 20% of the world's freshwater is in ONE river: the Amazon in South America.

20% of the world's surface freshwater is in ONE lake: Lake Baikal in Russia.

The world's water:

97%

completely undrinkable (seawater)

2% is frozen in icebergs.

Less than 1% is usable by people.

Of the rest, a huge percentage has already been polluted by humans.

KING OF BLING

The largest-ever gemstone yet found is a 1,182–pound (lb) emerald displayed in Hong Kong in 2009.

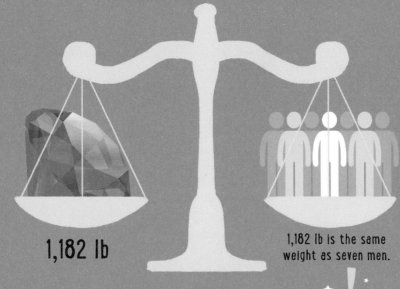

1,182 lb

1,182 lb is the same weight as seven men.

Diamonds are the most valuable gemstones. In 2010, a tiny pink diamond (just over 1 cm wide) was bought for £29 million ($46 million).

With $46 million you could buy:

A private jet

120 houses

Ten luxury yachts

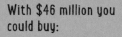

NO BUSINESS LIKE THROW BUSINESS

Since the dawn of time, human beings have thrown things at other human beings. But how far? And what weapons have they used?

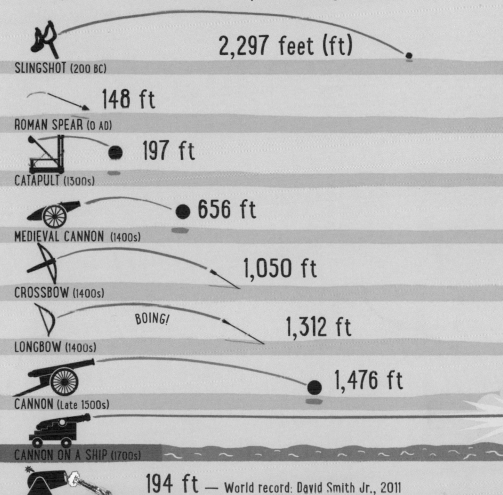

2,297 feet (ft)

SLINGSHOT (200 BC)

148 ft

ROMAN SPEAR (0 AD)

197 ft

CATAPULT (1300s)

656 ft

MEDIEVAL CANNON (1400s)

1,050 ft

CROSSBOW (1400s)

BOING!

1,312 ft

LONGBOW (1400s)

1,476 ft

CANNON (Late 1500s)

CANNON ON A SHIP (1700s)

194 ft — World record: David Smith Jr., 2011

MAN SHOT FROM CANNON (2000s)

SAY WHAT?

Some animals' names don't exactly make sense.

Woof!

A **prairie dog** is not a dog. It is a rodent.

A **flying fox** is not a fox. It is a bat.

A **polecat** is not a cat. It's more like a weasel.

A **horned toad** is not a toad. It's not even an amphibian. It's a lizard.

A **mongoose** is not a goose. It's more like a ferret.

5,249 ft

A **flying lemur** can't fly and it isn't a lemur.

An **oystercatcher** prefers mussels and other shellfish.

A **white rhino** is a rhino. But it isn't white. Not even a bit. It's gray.

A **sea monkey** is not a monkey. It's a type of shrimp.

Anteaters do occasionally eat ants. But they also enjoy termites.

AND FINALLY...

Oink!

A **guinea pig** is not from Guinea and it's definitely NOT a pig.

HOW MANY MAMMALS?

Did you know that in the last census there were 63 million people living in the UK? But what if we'd included every mammal, not just humans?*

Horses
1 million

Deer
1 million

Guinea pigs
1 million

Voles
100 million

Around a quarter of all mammals in the UK are voles.

Bats
4.9 million

Sheep
32 million

Shrews
54 million

People
63 million

Cats
8 million

Rats
6.8 million

Squeak!

*This is based on the latest government information. Usually they count animals in the winter.

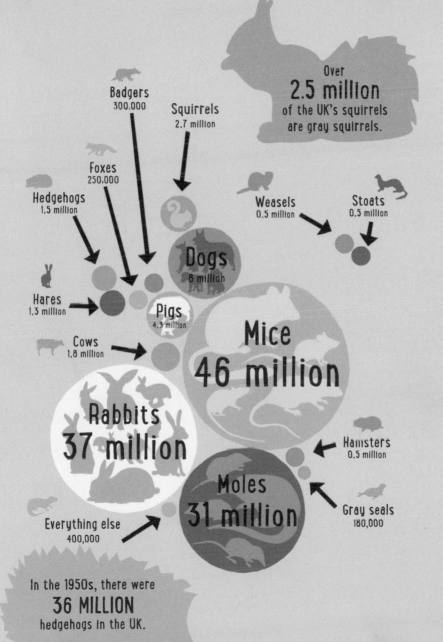

Over **2.5 million** of the UK's squirrels are gray squirrels.

Badgers 300,000

Squirrels 2.7 million

Foxes 250,000

Hedgehogs 1.5 million

Weasels 0.5 million

Stoats 0.5 million

Dogs 8 million

Hares 1.3 million

Pigs 4.3 million

Cows 1.8 million

Mice 46 million

Rabbits 37 million

Hamsters 0.5 million

Moles 31 million

Gray seals 180,000

Everything else 400,000

In the 1950s, there were **36 MILLION** hedgehogs in the UK.

IT CAME FROM OUTER SPACE

Two billion years ago, one of the largest meteors ever to hit Earth landed in Vredefort, South Africa. It created the world's biggest crater.

The meteor was traveling at 36,000 kmh* (22,370 mph**).

It was almost twice as big as the meteor that supposedly killed off the dinosaurs.

RUN!

*kilometers per hour **miles per hour

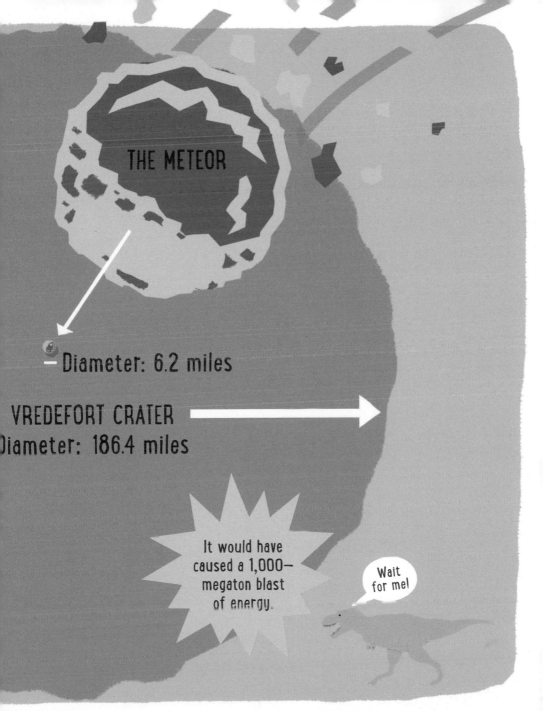

HOT STUFF

The Sun's energy is terrifying.

If you took exactly
THIS MUCH

of the Sun's energy...

...and placed
it in the
middle of
London...

...everyone in
THAT CIRCLE
would
DIE!

London

France

LEAVE ME BEE!

The most times a person has been stung by bees without dying:

PLANE CRAZY

In 1972, Vesna Vulovic fell 33,333 feet (ft) from an airplane and survived...

But how far exactly is 33,333 ft?

Vesna Vulovic
33,333 ft

Mount Everest
29,029 ft

Bald eagle
14,764 ft

Average skydiving height
12,500 ft
(Unlike Vesna Vulovic, skydivers have parachutes!)

Cumulus clouds
3,281 ft

World's tallest building
(Burj Khalifa)
Over 2,717 ft

MOSTLY ARMLESS

Think you need a pair of hands to pick things up? Think again. Dong Changsheng pulled a 3,307-pound car 33 feet with ropes connected to his eyelids in 2006.

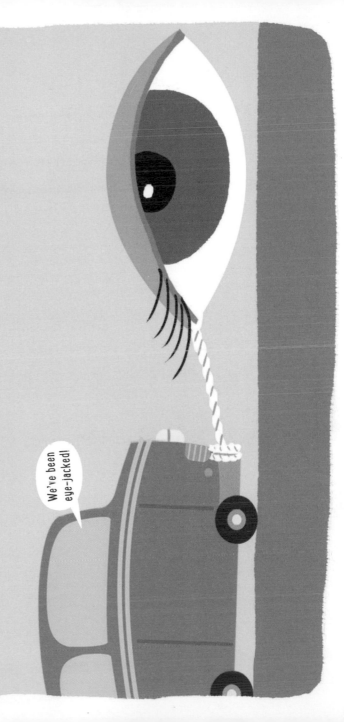

LAWS YOU MIGHT NOT KNOW

Here are some laws you've probably never heard of...

 **In Iceland,** everyone has to learn to swim by law.

In Russia, it is illegal to brush your teeth more than twice a day.

 **In London,** it is against the law to jump the line in a tube station.

In Samoa, it is illegal for a man to forget his wife's birthday.

In Oklahoma, it is illegal to make faces at a dog.

In the UK, you are not allowed to handle salmon suspiciously.

In Thailand, it is against the law to leave the house without underwear.

In Portugal, it is illegal to pee in the sea.

In the UK, it is illegal to enter the Houses of Parliament wearing a suit of armor.

NATURAL BORN KILLERS

Many animals are deadly to humans. But which are the deadliest?

Each individual animal has enough venom in it to kill...

Inland taipan

Box jellyfish

Puffer fish

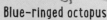

Blue-ringed octopus

King cobra

Cone snail

※ = antidote available

※ 100 people

※ 60 people

30 people

25 people

※ 20 people

20 people

GO, GO, GO!

How often do different animals need to poo?

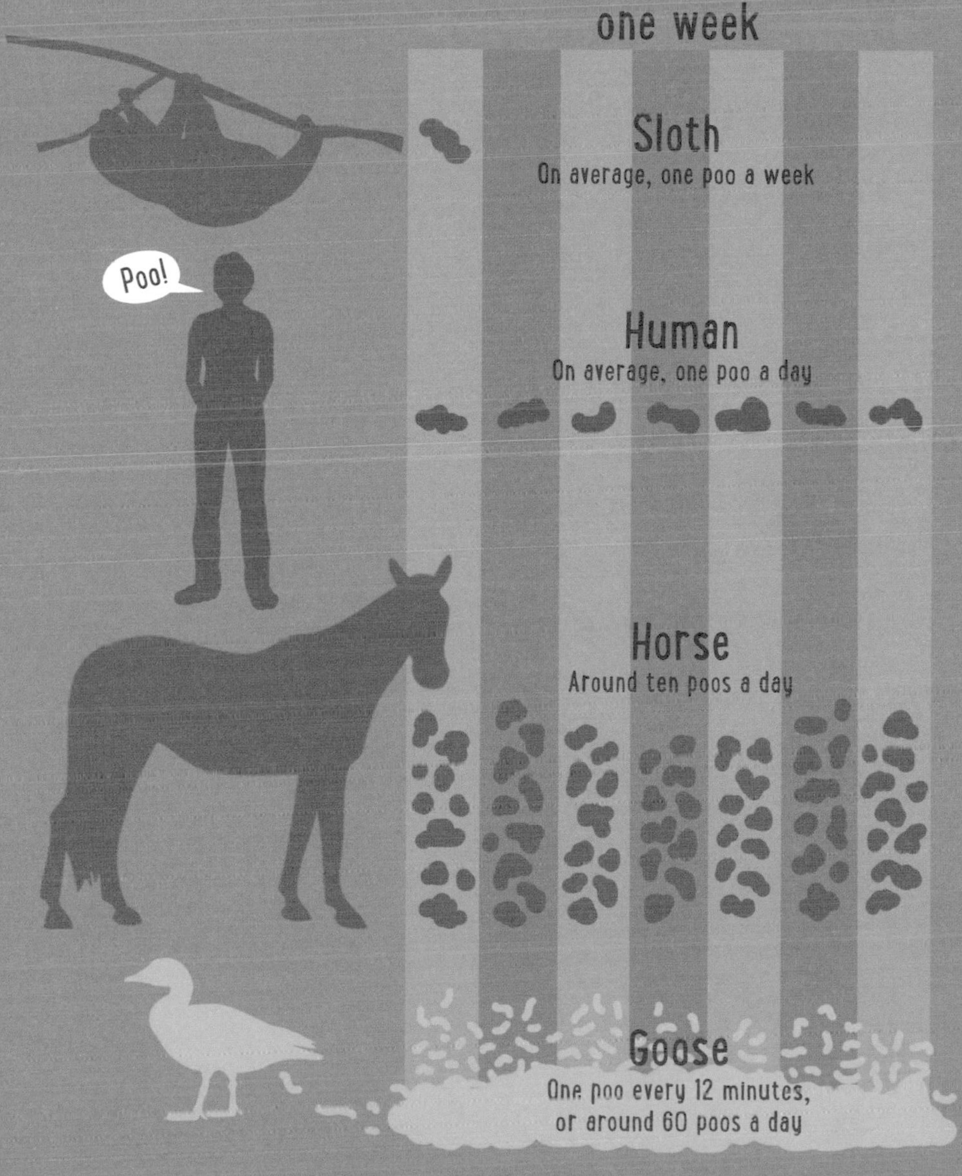

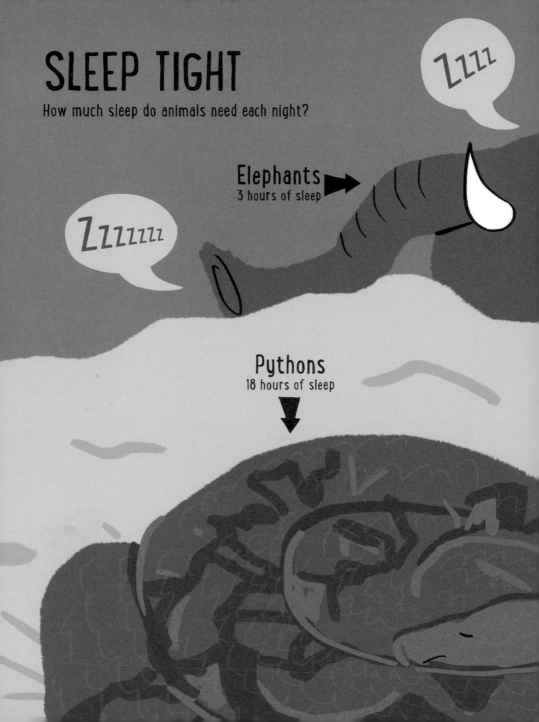

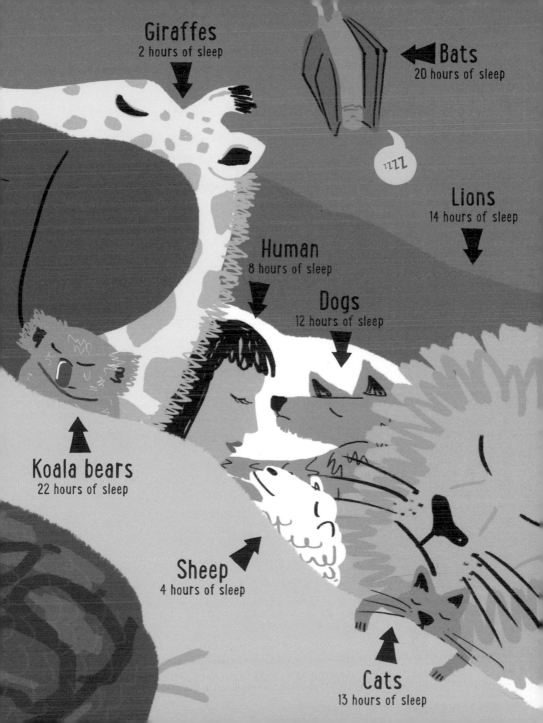

SIGHT FOR SORE EYES

As cities grow in size, air pollution can be an eye-wateringly large problem.

In 1940, visibility in Mexico City was 62 miles.

In 2000, visibility in Mexico City was 1 mile.

WHAT A LOAD OF GARBAGE!

There are millions of pieces of space junk in the atmosphere, caused by satellites crashing, rockets disintegrating, weapons exploding, and a hundred other causes.

Oh no!

22,000
pieces of space junk are more than 4 inches wide.

The weirdest is a wrench dropped from the International Space Station.

The biggest is the size of a washing machine.

Almost two thirds
of the most dangerous space junk was created by explosions: a satellite being blown up in 2007 and two satellites colliding in 2009.

Most space junk travels at
4.5 miles per second or roughly
16,200 mph.

A single fleck of paint traveling
at this speed can cause
the same damage as a

**grand piano
traveling
at 60 mph.**

The International Space Station
has to constantly steer
around space junk.

On average, a piece of
space junk falls to Earth
every day. Nobody has been
hit by space junk...yet!

HEAVY LIFTING

The largest plane in the world, the An-225, was originally designed to lift the Russian space shuttle. Now it's used as a cargo plane in the Ukraine.

The An-225 can carry **330 tons** of fuel. That could fill the tanks of 7,500 cars!

Fasten your seat belts.

32 landing wheels

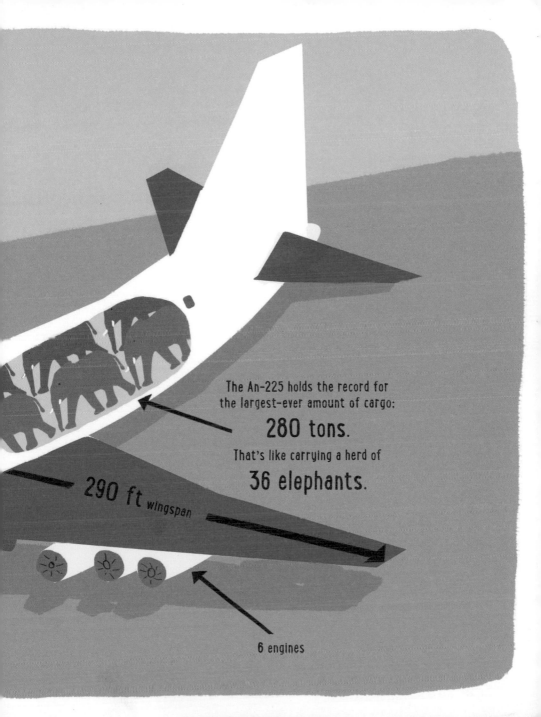

The An-225 holds the record for
the largest-ever amount of cargo:

280 tons.

That's like carrying a herd of

36 elephants.

290 ft wingspan

6 engines

THAT'S A WRAP!

It took more than 4,000 square feet (ft²) of bandages to make a mummy.

Tennis court
2,808 ft²

Sheet for super king-size bed
92 ft²

A saltwater crocodile
21 ft

A (very large) python
32 ft

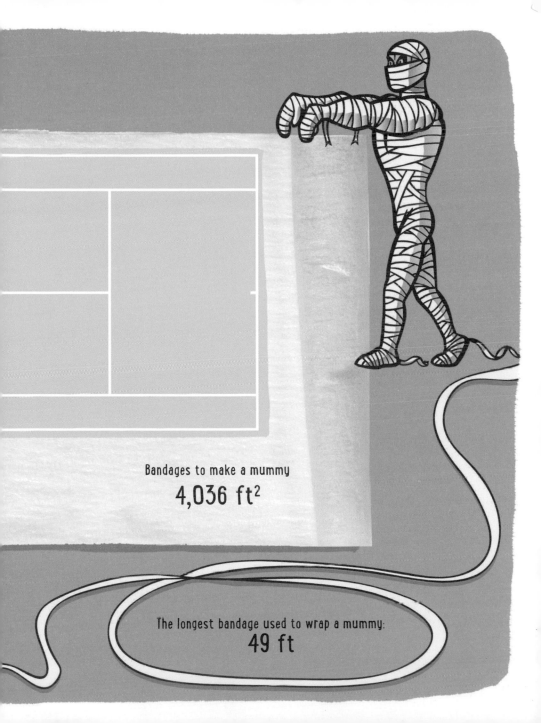

Bandages to make a mummy

4,036 ft²

The longest bandage used to wrap a mummy:

49 ft

LET US PREY

The rabbit is thought to be the most preyed-upon animal in the world. Here's a selection of the predators that target rabbits.

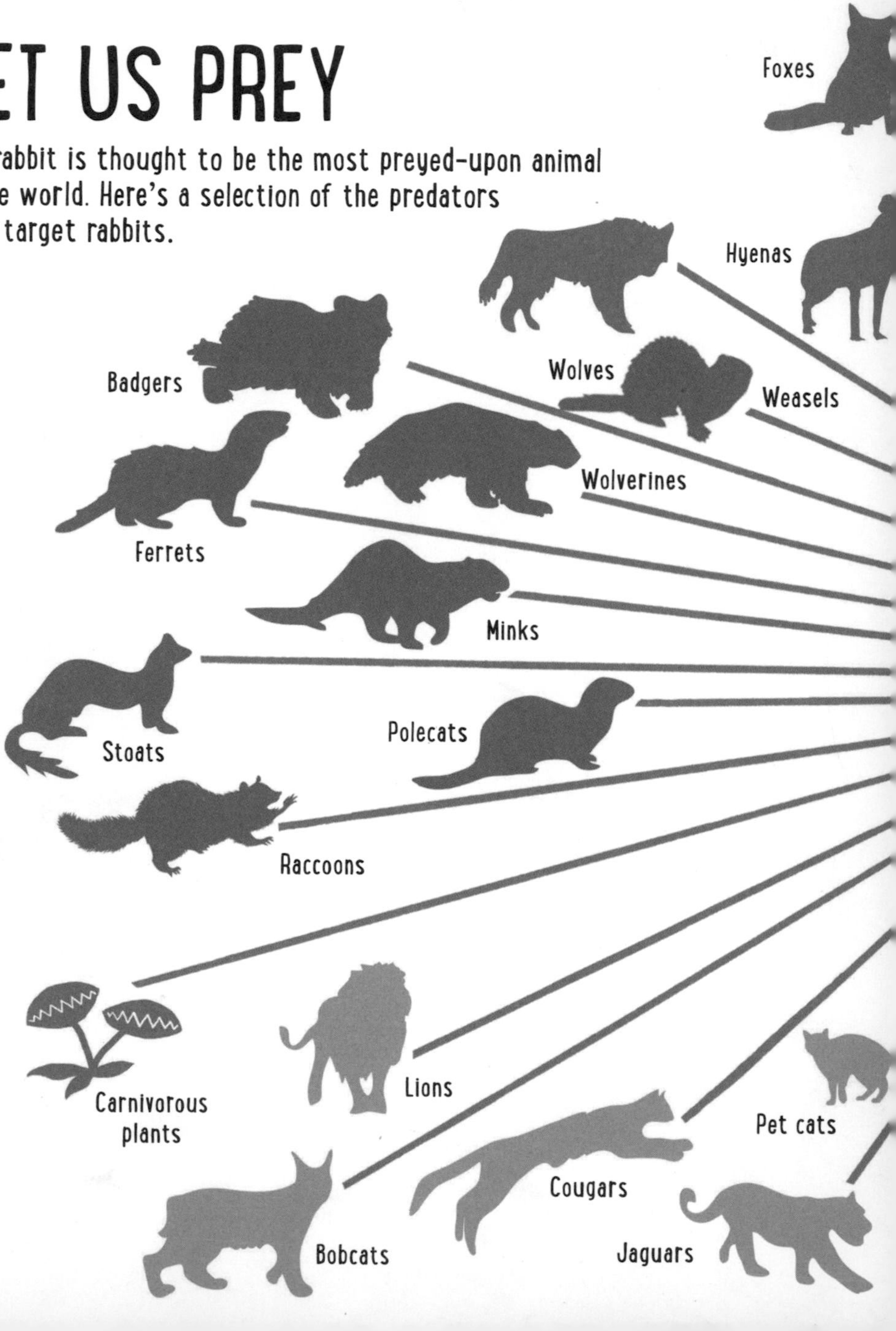

Foxes

Hyenas

Badgers

Wolves

Weasels

Wolverines

Ferrets

Minks

Stoats

Polecats

Raccoons

Carnivorous plants

Lions

Pet cats

Bobcats

Cougars

Jaguars

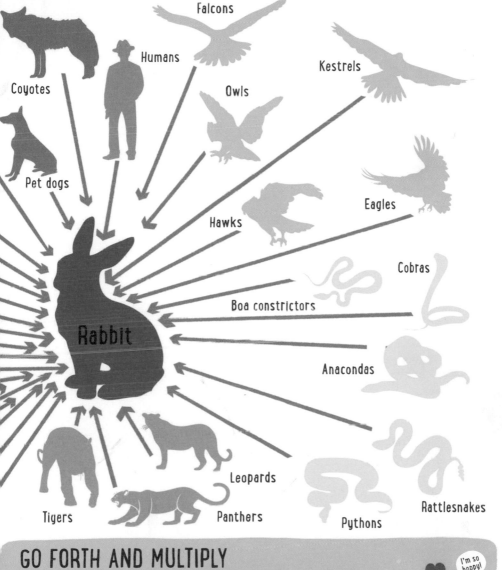

GO FORTH AND MULTIPLY

Fortunately rabbits are very good at having babies and replacing their fallen friends. For example, before 1788, there were no rabbits in Australia. Then in 1788, five rabbits arrived on a boat from England.

By 1950, there were 600 million rabbits in Australia.

One pair of rabbits can produce 60 babies a year.

STINGING IN THE RAIN

Many weird animals and objects have fallen from the skies, including jellyfish...

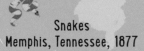

Pennies and halfpennies
Hanham, UK, 1966

Snakes
Memphis, Tennessee, 1877

Jellyfish
Bath, UK, 1894

Ow!

Worms
Jennings, Louisiana, 2007

Golf balls
Punta Gorda, Florida, 1969

Spiders
Salta Province, Argentina, 2007

Orange snow
Siberia, Russia, 2012

Frogs
Ishikawa Prefecture,
Japan, 2009

Dead birds
Faenza, Italy, 2011

Diamonds
Okay, this has never
happened on Earth.
But scientists
believe that it rains
diamonds on
both Uranus and
Neptune!

Red rain
Kerala, India, 2012

Fish
Philippines, 2012

UNDER PRESSURE

As you get deeper in the sea, the water around you puts more pressure on your body. But how much more?

700 ft
Farthest ever reached by a freediver (someone just taking a deep breath). The pressure shrinks the lungs to the size of lemons.

8,202 ft
The pressure here is what your little toe would feel like if a hippo stood on it. But on every inch of your body.

12,415 ft
The wreck of the *Titanic* is here. According to one diver, the water pressure makes it look like it's been squashed by a giant's fist.

16,404 ft
Anglerfish and cusk eels live near the seabed. They have adapted to avoid being crushed by the water around them. For example, the anglerfish has a skeleton made of cartilage (which is flexible and squeezable) rather than bone (which isn't).

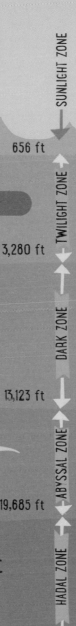

SUNLIGHT ZONE

656 ft

TWILIGHT ZONE

2,400 ft
A modern submarine has a "crush depth" of about 2,400 feet. This is when the water pressure will start to crush its metal sides.

3,280 ft

9,842 ft
The deepest a whale can dive.

DARK ZONE

13,123 ft

Glug!

13,123 ft
Here the pressure is almost 6,000 lb per square inch. That's like being crushed alive in the jaws of a T. Rex.

ABYSSAL ZONE

19,685 ft

around 36,000 ft
At the bottom of the sea, the pressure is like having 50 jumbo jets on top of you.

HADAL ZONE

around 36,000 ft

RAIN CHECK

In 2005, Mumbai had 37 inches (in.) of rain in a single day—the most ever recorded. But how much is 37 inches?

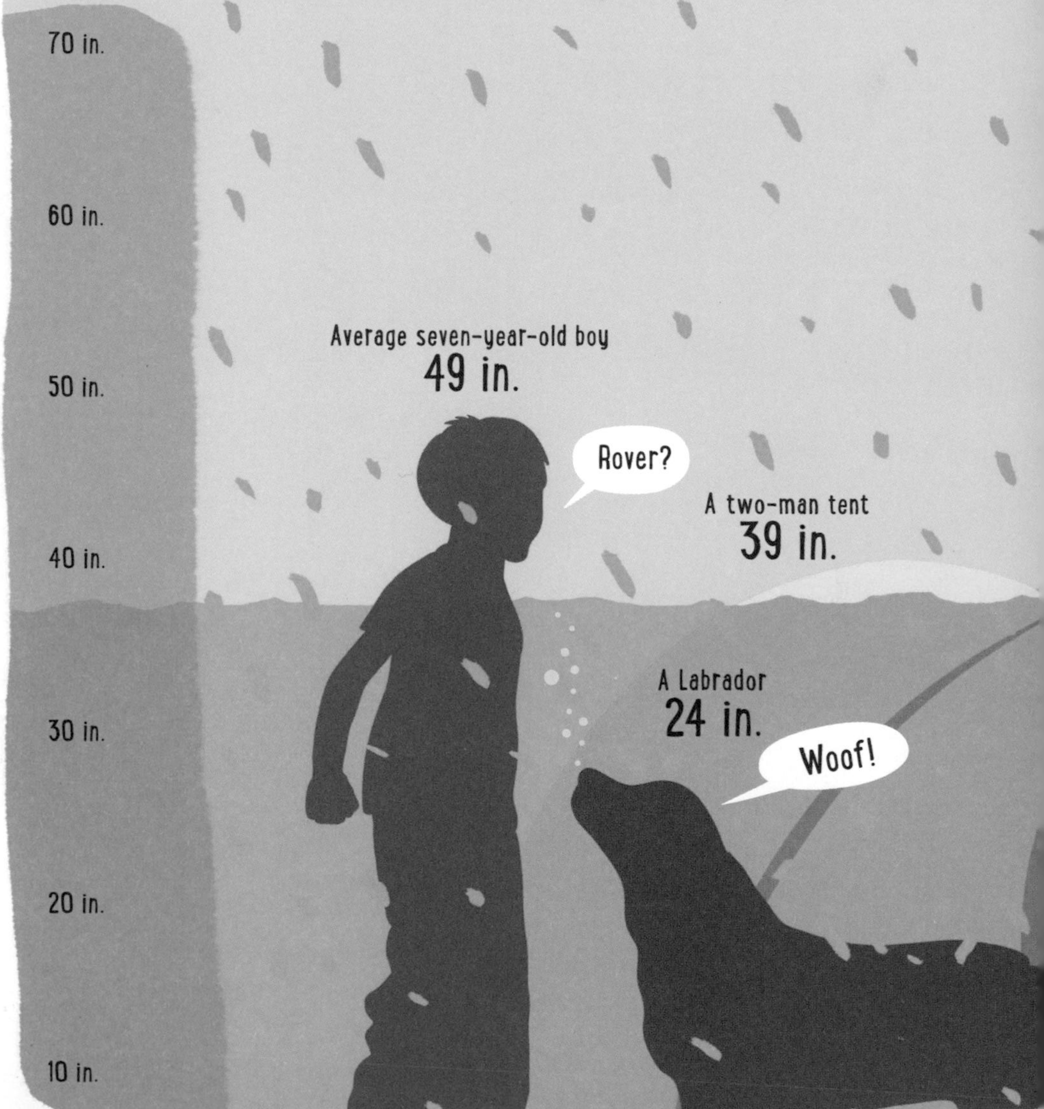

Average front door
80 in.

Corn on the cob
(maize plant)
61 in.

12 mice standing on each
other's shoulders
38.6 in

ALL SHAPES AND SIZES

What are the longest, largest, and most spectacular animals ever discovered?

Average adult
male (UK) — standing up
5.7 feet (ft)

An eagle's nest (or aerie) can be
up to **18 ft** deep.

Saltwater crocodile
21 ft

A baby blue whale is about
26 ft long—the
longest and largest baby in the natural world!

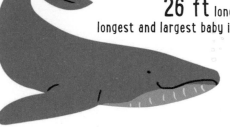

Reticulated python
33 ft

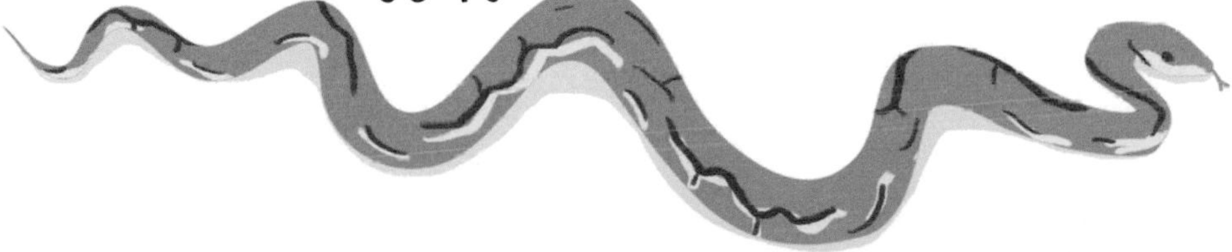

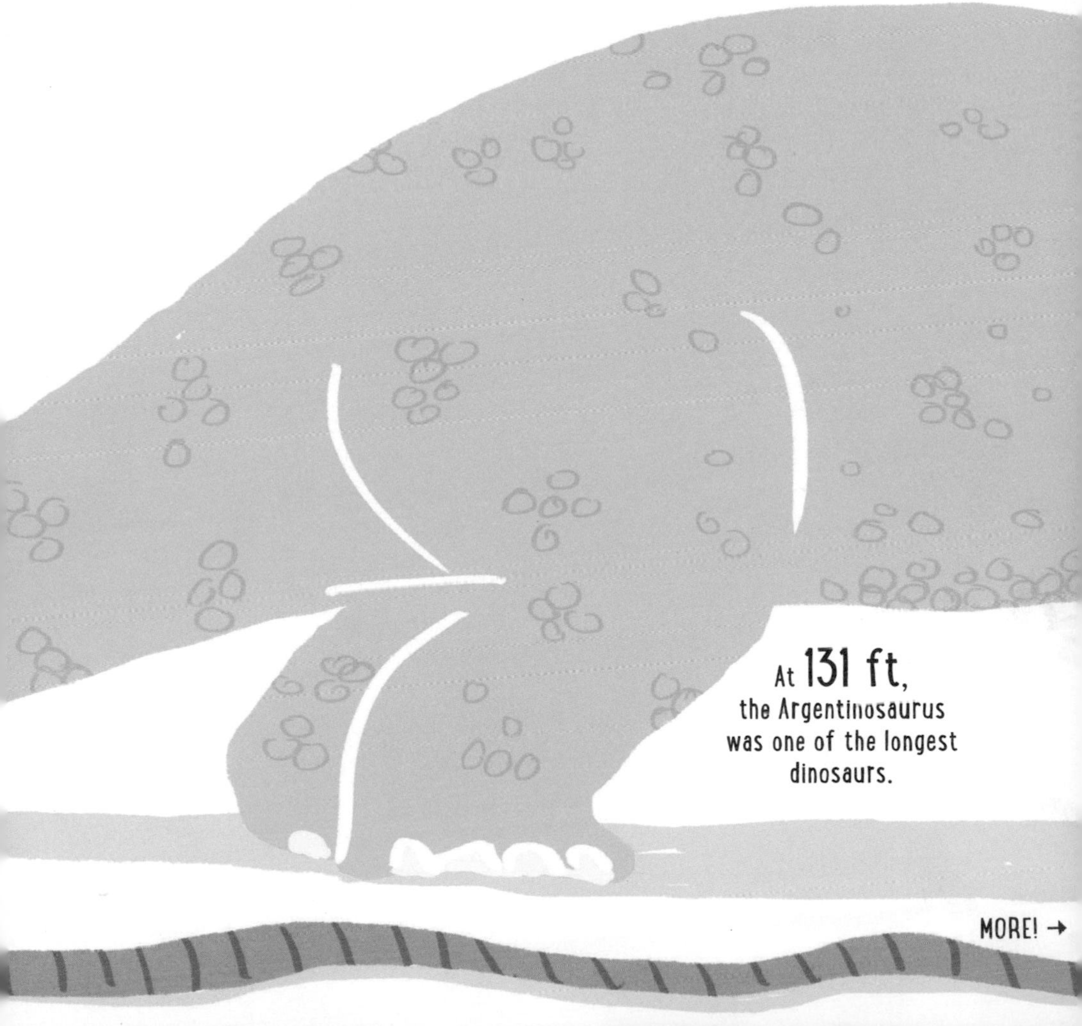

At **131 ft**,
the Argentinosaurus
was one of the longest
dinosaurs.

MORE! →

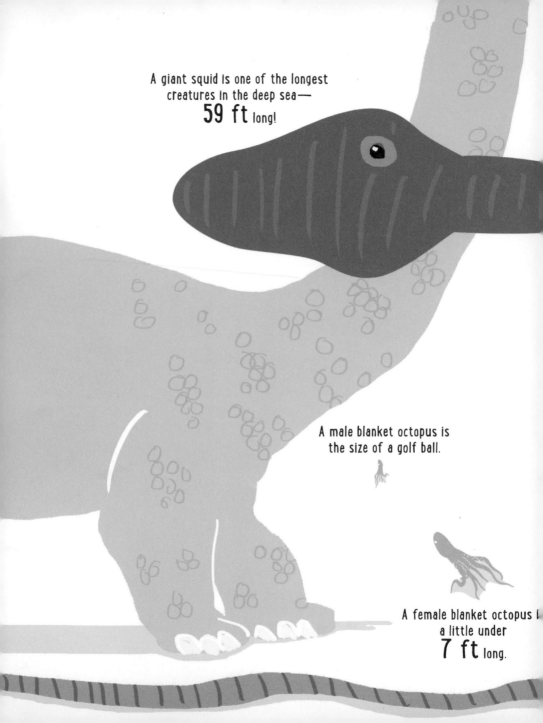

A giant squid is one of the longest creatures in the deep sea—
59 ft long!

A male blanket octopus is the size of a golf ball.

A female blanket octopus i
a little under
7 ft long.

An albatross has the longest wingspan of any bird—**11.5 ft**

A narwhal has the longest tooth in the animal kingdom—over **10 ft** long!

A rocket frog can jump almost **7 ft** (50 times its body length). This is like you being able to leap halfway along a football field—in a single jump!

EVEN MORE! →

IT'LL NEVER WORK...

When two different species have a baby, it's known as a hybrid. But what are the hybrids called?

A male lion

A female tiger

A liger

When the father is a tiger and the mother a lion, the baby is known as a tigon.

A male zebra

A female donkey

A zonkey

A male horse and a female zebra can also breed. Their baby is known as a hebra.

COUNTDOWN

Things that happened as you read this sentence...*

Your body just made
30 million new cells.

Twelve babies
were born.

Around 10,000 tons of water
flowed over Niagara Falls.

Earth flew 55 miles
through space.

A hummingbird flapped
its wings 240 times.

The world's fastest car, the
Ariel Atom, accelerated from
0 to 60 mph.

Light from the Sun just
traveled half a million
miles toward Earth.

An area of Amazon rain forest
the size of three football fields
just got chopped down.

People used Google to search
the internet almost half
a million times.

Lightning struck the Earth
300 times.

*...assuming it took you 3 seconds to read it.

STEVE THE SQUIRREL'S SECRET TREASURE MAP

A squirrel can remember the location of up to 10,000 buried nuts!

FROM TINY ACORNS...
As well as the 10,000 they remember, squirrels also FORGET where HALF of their nuts are buried. Many of these grow into trees.

AIN'T NOTHING
BUT A HOT DOG

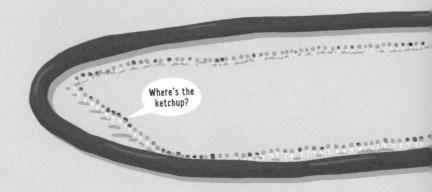

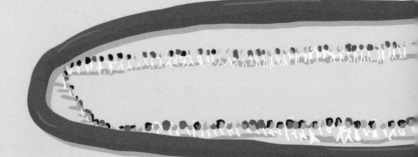

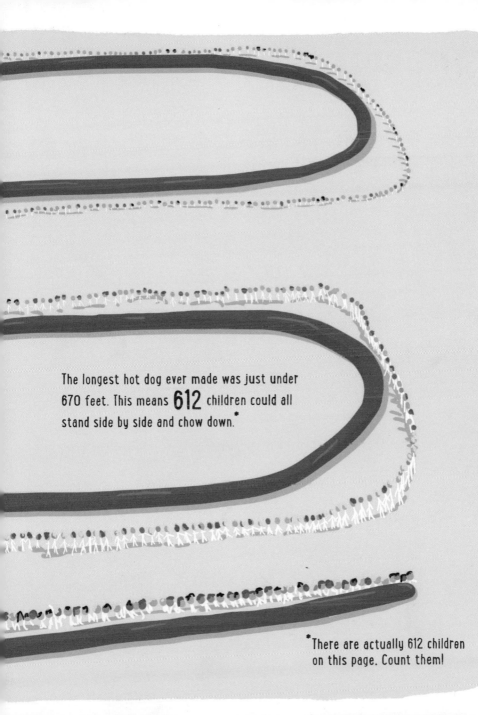

The longest hot dog ever made was just under 670 feet. This means **612** children could all stand side by side and chow down.*

*There are actually 612 children on this page. Count them!

STILL HUNGRY?

Biggest-ever pancake
49 feet (ft) wide

Biggest-ever fruitcake
30 ft
460 baking trays were
used to bake it!

Longest-ever kebab
26 ft

Biggest-ever
hamburger
24 ft wide

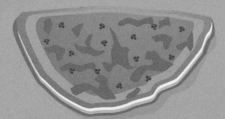

Biggest-ever omelet
39 ft wide

A crowd of 3,500 people came to
watch the burger being cooked.
It took 2 hours.

Biggest-ever doughnut
20 ft wide

Biggest-ever chocolate bar
13 ft wide and **13 ft** long
It weighed nearly 6 tons.

Biggest-ever pizza
123 ft wide*

*The pizza was made in Norwood, South Africa, by Norwood Hypermarket in 1990

THUNDERSTRUCK

Roy Sullivan was a park ranger in Virginia. He holds the world record for being struck by lightning more times than any other human being: SEVEN TIMES.* But when, how, and where did this happen?

1972
In a ranger station—
Hair was burned off.

1969
While driving a truck—
Eyebrows, eyelashes,
and some of his hair
were burned off.

1977
Fishing—Head, chest,
and stomach were
burned.

1942
Hiding in a fire
lookout tower—
Strip was burned
along his right leg.

1970
In his front yard—
Left shoulder was
burned.

1973
On patrol in the park—
Left arm, left leg,
and right leg were
burned. Left shoe was
blasted off.

1976
On patrol in the park—
Ankle was burned.

*
All seven lightning strikes
were verified by doctors.

On another occasion, Roy Sullivan was almost hit by lightning
while helping his wife hang the laundry out in their back garden.
But this time, the lightning missed him and hit his wife instead.

FOLLOW YOUR NOSE

In 1925, a police dog picked up the scent of a sheep thief on the edge of the Great Karoo desert in South Africa. By following the scent, he finally caught up with the thief—100 MILES LATER!

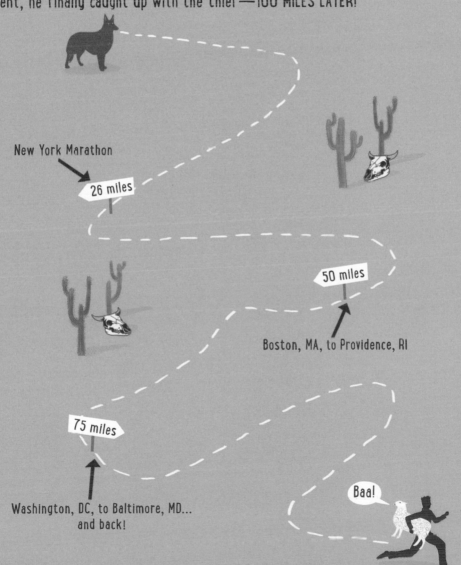

New York Marathon

26 miles

50 miles

Boston, MA, to Providence, RI

75 miles

Washington, DC, to Baltimore, MD... and back!

Baa!

WHAT A LIGHTWEIGHT!

How much would the average man weigh on different planets?
It depends on how big the planet is and how far he is from
the center of the planet.

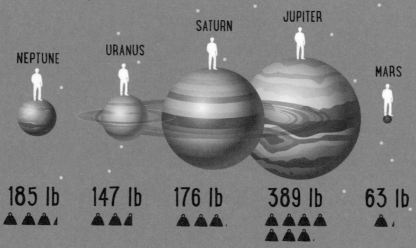

NEPTUNE
185 lb

URANUS
147 lb

SATURN
176 lb

JUPITER
389 lb

MARS
63 lb

= 55 lb

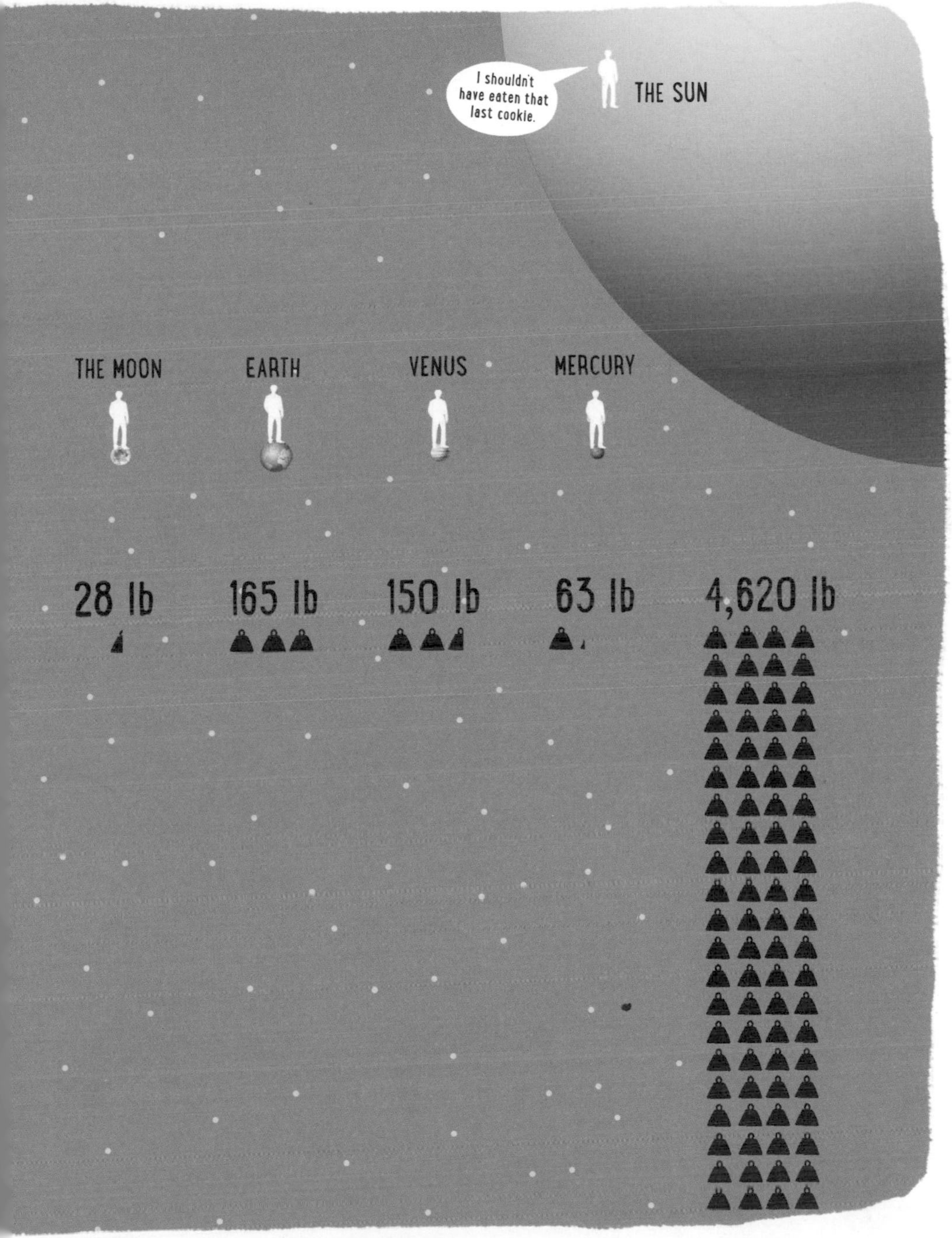
I shouldn't have eaten that last cookie.
THE SUN
THE MOON
EARTH
VENUS
MERCURY
28 lb
165 lb
150 lb
63 lb
4,620 lb

YOU COULDN'T MAKE IT UP...

The playwright William Shakespeare invented over 1,000 new words—more than any other author.* How many of these words do you know?

Eyeball

Puking

Belongings

Archvillain

Elbow

Mountaineer

Manager

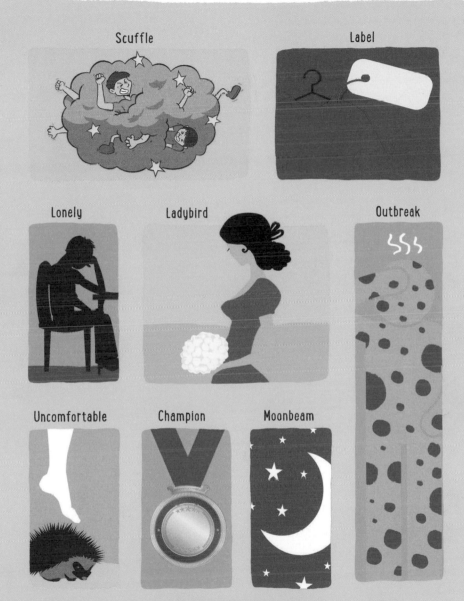

Scuffle

Label

Lonely

Ladybird

Outbreak

Uncomfortable

Champion

Moonbeam

*By invented, we mean he was one of the first people to write the words down or use them in public. People probably said them before—or they wouldn't have understood what Shakespeare was talking about.

ZOOM!

What's the zoom on your camera like? Bet it's not as good as a spy satellite. These cameras are 250 miles up in the sky, orbiting the Earth. And their zoom lens is INCREDIBLE.

ZOOMED OUT

ZOOMED IN

DRIVEN TO SUCCEED

A driver in Long Island, NY, has driven his car—a Volvo P1800—
3 MILLION MILES. This is a world record! But how far is 3 million miles?

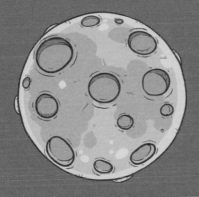

He could have driven to
the Moon and back

6 TIMES.

Distance from the
Earth to the Moon =

238,855 miles

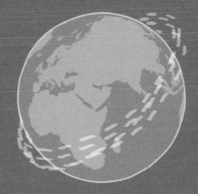

He could have driven around
the Earth 120 TIMES.

Circumference of Earth =

25,000 miles

He could have driven across
America coast-to-coast

1,434 times.

Distance from
San Diego to Jacksonville =

2,336 miles

LOUDER THAN WORDS

Using the right body language in the wrong place could land you in hot water...

Nodding 	Bulgaria	Rest of the world
	No	Yes

Shaking hands 	Asia	Rest of the world
	Very rude	Very friendly

Eye contact 	US/Europe	South America/Middle East/Asia
	Very polite (I'm interested in what you're saying.)	Very rude (I'm staring at you.)

Eyes closed 	US/Europe	China/Japan
	Very rude (I'm bored by what you're saying.)	Very polite (I'm thinking hard about what you're saying.)

HELLO, MOM!

Which are the most popular days to make international phone calls?

 ## 1.Mother's Day
4th Sunday of Lent

 ## 2.New Year's Day
January 1st

 ## 3.Valentine's Day
February 14th

Mothers do okay for cards on Mother's Day, too. Particularly when compared to fathers!

Number of cards sold in an average year:

Mother's Day	152 MILLION
Father's Day	95 MILLION

BANG! BANG!

Fireworks come in all shapes and sizes...

The longest-ever firework

← **2 miles long** →

That's as long as 35 soccer fields!

The biggest-ever rocket

23 ft tall

The biggest-ever Catherine wheel

105 ft wide

Some of the best-known firework shapes

The PEONY is the most common type of firework. It's named after the famous flower.

The WILLOW has long burning stars that make the firework look like a weeping willow.

The PALM bursts with large trails, making the firework look like a palm tree.

The DIADEM has a central cluster of stars that don't move, making the firework look like a crown.

MADE IN CHINA

90% of the world's fireworks are made in China.

More than half of the world's fireworks are made in ONE PLACE in China—Liuyang.

Boo!

The Chinese invented fireworks in around 600 AD. They were originally designed to scare off evil sprits.

LET'S GET ROLLING

Ever wondered where you can find the world's longest or fastest roller coaster?

Tate Modern,
London
325 ft

St. Paul's Cathedral,
364 ft

Big Ben
315 ft

Ferrari Enzo
0–60 in 3.14 second

Formula Rossa roller coaster, Abu Dha
0–60 in 2 seconds

The longest roller coaster

The roller coaster in Nagashima Spa Land, Japan, is 8,137 ft long.

3 minutes

Whee!

4 minutes

2 minutes

1 minute

It takes over 4 minutes to get to the end. If you started boiling an egg when you got on, it would be ready to eat by the time you got off!

The tallest roller coaster

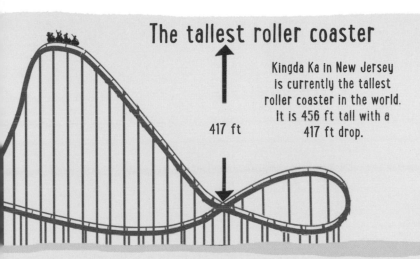

417 ft

Kingda Ka in New Jersey is currently the tallest roller coaster in the world. It is 456 ft tall with a 417 ft drop.

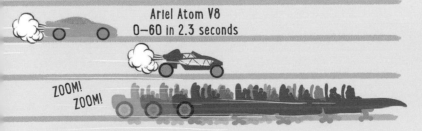

Porsche 911 Turbo
0–60 in 2.7 seconds

Ariel Atom V8
0–60 in 2.3 seconds

ZOOM!
ZOOM!

The fastest roller coaster

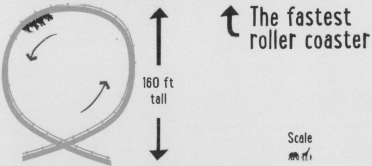

160 ft tall

Scale

The tallest vertical-loop roller coaster

Passengers on the Full Throttle roller coaster, Valencia, California.

NO WAY BACK

GOING...
1,000–5,000 left in the wild

Giant panda

Tiger

Galapagos penguin

Ganges River dolphin

GOING...
Fewer than 1,000 left in the wild

Mountain gorilla

Yangtze finless porpoise

Black-footed ferret

Mekong giant catfish

GONE
Extinct

Irish elk
These animals were almost 7 ft tall, but their incredible antlers measured up to 12 ft tip to tip.

Elephant bird
At 10 ft, these huge birds were twice the size of a man. Extinct since the 1700s.

Steller's sea cow
This amazing sea creature was 30 ft long and weighed around 10 tons.

We all know that dinosaurs are extinct. But there are animals that used to share the planet with humans—and now they are gone forever. What were these animals and which animals may soon be joining them?

Sumatran elephant

Black rhino

African wild dog

Snow leopard

Vaquita porpoise

Cross River gorilla

Javan rhino

Amur leopard

Passenger pigeon

In 1500, there were 5 billion passenger pigeons in the US. 400 years later, there were none.

As dead as a ...

Dodo

The most famous extinct animal of all lived on the island of Mauritius until humans killed or ate them all.

Quagga

This zebra-like animal had brown and white stripes on the front half of its body. Extinct since 1883.

LET'S GO

There are 1,140 Lego bricks on this page, and the latest figures show that, across the world, people buy this many Lego bricks every SECOND!

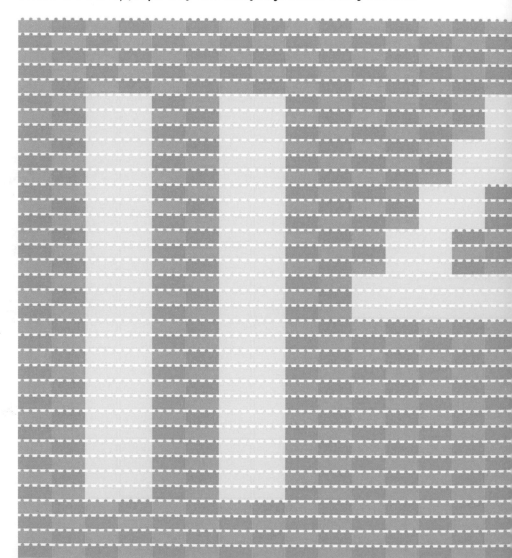

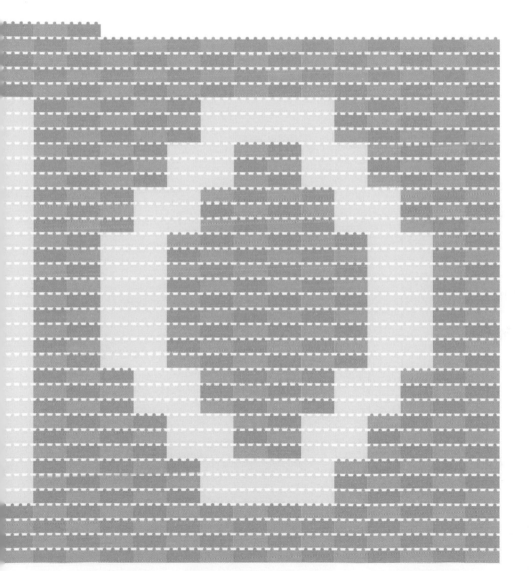

HAIR WE GO

How fast does the average person's hair grow?

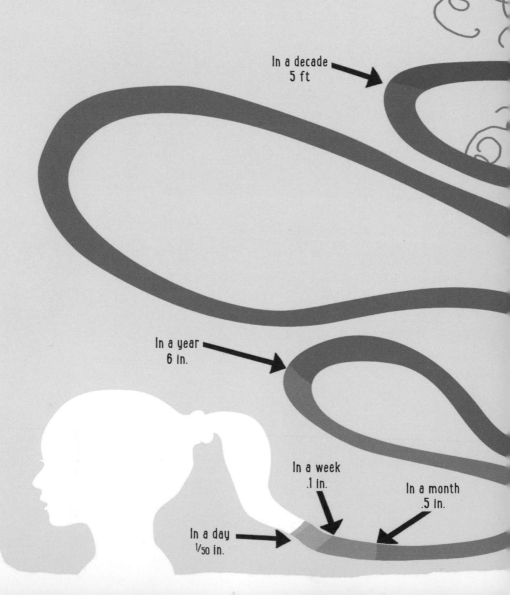

In a decade
5 ft

In a year
6 in.

In a week
.1 in.

In a month
.5 in.

In a day
1/50 in.

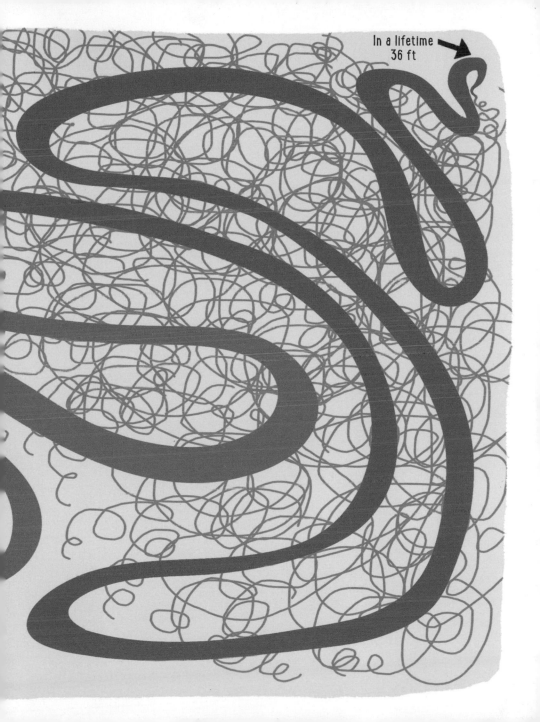

In a lifetime
36 ft

TOO HOT TO HANDLE?

How hot is that chili pepper? The Scoville scale can tell you...

Scoville heat units

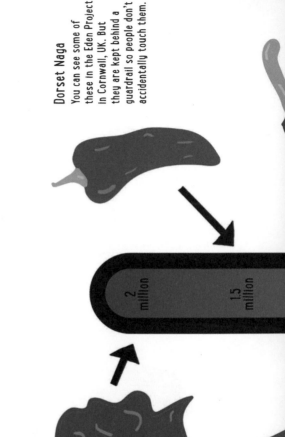

Carolina Reaper
This fiery demon holds the record for the hottest chili in the world. If you ate a whole one, you would almost certainly end up in a hospital.

Infinity Chili
This chili is called "Infinity" because of its "never-ending" heat.

Dorset Naga
You can see some of these in the Eden Project in Cornwall, UK. But they are kept behind a guardrail so people don't accidentally touch them.

2 million

1.5 million

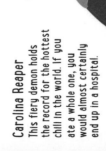

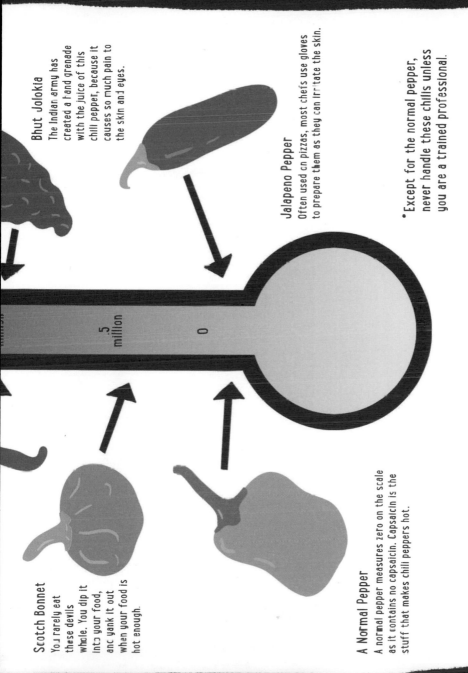

Bhut Jolokia
The Indian army has created a hand grenade with the juice of this chili pepper, because it causes so much pain to the skin and eyes.

Jalapeno Pepper
Often used on pizzas, most chefs use gloves to prepare them as they can irritate the skin.

* Except for the normal pepper, never handle these chilis unless you are a trained professional.

.5 million

0

Scotch Bonnet
You rarely eat these devils whole. You dip it into your food, and yank it out when your food is hot enough.

A Normal Pepper
A normal pepper measures zero on the scale as it contains no capsaicin. Capsaicin is the stuff that makes chili peppers hot.

LEFT RIGHT, LEFT RIGHT

In some regions—like the UK—people drive cars on the left side of the road. In others, they drive on the right. But what do MOST countries do?

54 countries drive on the left

142 countries drive on the right.

Arctic Ocean

North Pacific Ocean

Asia

North Pacific Ocean

Oceania

Indian Ocean

Europe

Africa

South Atlantic Ocean

North Atlantic Ocean

South America

North America

South Pacific Ocean

Arctic Ocean

North Pacific Ocean

LOOK WHO'S TALKING

What are the most widely spoken languages in the world?
And how many people speak them?

Hello
English—328 million

你好
Mandarin Chinese—845 million

Hola
Spanish—329 million

नमस्ते
Hindi—182 million

مرحباً
Arabic—221 million

Olá
Portuguese—178 million

привет
Russian—144 million

সলাম
Bengali—181 million

TAKE TWO

Over HALF of the world speaks TWO OR
MORE languages on a daily basis. How many
languages do you speak?

OLDEST SPECIES

Some animal species have been around for a very long time...

400 MILLION YEARS

Coelacanth (400 million years)
Previously thought to have been wiped out 100 million years ago, coelacanths were rediscovered in the 1930s and are seen as a "living fossil" as they haven't changed in almost 400 million years.

Lamprey (360 million years)
Many lampreys use their sharp teeth to drill into the flesh of other fish and drink their blood. This ruthless way of staying alive is one of the reasons they've lasted for over 300 million years.

150 MILLION YEARS

Frilled shark (150 million years)
This deepwater shark attacks like a snake—coiling its body back and then lunging forward. Its long jaws mean it can swallow prey whole. It first appeared on Earth about the same time as the Diplodocus—but it's still here...

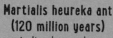

Martialis heureka ant (120 million years)
The ants live deep underground and are completely blind.

50 MILLION YEARS

100 MILLION YEARS

O MILLION YEARS

300 MILLION YEARS

Horseshoe crab (200 million years)
Closely related to spiders and scorpions, these crabs have an incredibly hard shell and five pairs of legs—four of which have sharp claws at the tip.

Tadpole shrimp (220 million years)
Also described as living fossils, these shrimp live anywhere there is shallow water: rock pools, ponds, estuaries, streams, bogs, or moorland. They also eat anything and everything.

250 MILLION YEARS

O MILLION YEARS

Tuatara (250 million years)
The tuatara is a New Zealand reptile with a frilled head. Like lizards, it can grow a new tail if a predator bites one off.

Humans (200,000 years)

NOW

Snapping turtle (40 million years)
Snapping turtles cannot hide in their shells like other turtles. This is why they "snap" their jaws when attacked.

HOW DO YOU SLEEP?

According to one study, most people sleep in one of six positions. But which is the most common? And how do you sleep?

1. The Fetus
41% sleep in this position. These people are said to be tough on the outside but sensitive on the inside.

2. The Log
15% sleep in this position. These people are meant to be loyal and trusting.

3. The Yearner
13% sleep in this position. These people can be suspicious and stubborn—they rarely change their minds.

4. The Soldier
8% sleep in this position. These people are said to be quiet and reserved. They are also more likely to snore.

5. Freefall
7% sleep in this position. These people are outgoing and sociable, but don't like being told off or criticized.

6. The Starfish
5% sleep in this position. These people are open, friendly, and helpful.

DREAM ON

When you're asleep, what do you dream about?
Here are the five most common dreams.

1. Being chased

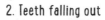

2. Teeth falling out

4. Being unprepared
for an exam

3. Desperate to use
the bathroom

5. Falling

WHAT RECORDS WILL YOU BREAK?

Just because you're young, it doesn't mean you can't be a record breaker.

At the age of 4, Dorothy Straight became the youngest person ever to publish a book. It was called *How the World Began* and it also included Dorothy's pictures.

At 6, Luis Tanner became the youngest-ever TV presenter. His show *Cooking for Kids with Luis* was first aired in October 2004.

When he was 8, Kim Ung-Yong got a job with NASA. He also became a doctor at the age of 15.

4 5 6 7 8 9 10

By the age of 5, Eleanor Gamble had sunk a hole-in-one. She was playing in the 2010 Easter Pairs competition in Cambridge Lakes, England.

By the time she was 7, Connie Talbot had an album in the UK charts. It was called *Over the Rainbow* and it was released in 2007.

By the age of 9, Kishan Shrikanth had made a feature film. It was called *Care of Footpath* and it was about an orphaned boy who dreams of going to school.

At 10 years old, Tatum O'Neal won an Oscar. It was for a film called *Paper Moon*. The film also starred her father.

When he was 12, Sergey Karjakin became a chess grandmaster. He had started playing chess at the age of 5.

At the age of 14, Michael Perham sailed across the Atlantic Ocean by himself. His boat was called *Cheeky Monkey*.

11 **12** **13** **14** **15**

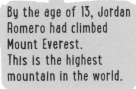

By the age of 11, Thomas Gregory had swum the English Channel. It took him 11 hours and 54 minutes.

By the age of 13, Jordan Romero had climbed Mount Everest. This is the highest mountain in the world.

When he was 15, Reuben Noble-Lazarus became the youngest-ever player in an English league soccer match. He came on as a substitute for Barnsley in September 2008.

WHAT DID YOU CALL ME?

Kings and noblemen often have nicknames.
But who was called what?

The FAT

Alfonso II of Portugal	Charles III, Holy Roman Emperor	Conan II, Duke of Brittany	Henry I of Cyprus	Henry I of Navarre	Louis VI of France	Sancho I of Leon

The MAD

Charles VI of France	George III of Great Britain	Joanna of Castile	Ludwig II of Bavaria

The BALD

Charles II of France	Baldwin II, Count of Flanders	Idwal ab Anarawd of Gwynedd

The DRUNKARD

Michael III, Byzantine Emperor	Selim II, Ottoman Emperor	Wenceslaus, King of the Romans

Burp!

The SILENT

Shh! Olav III of Norway — William I of Orange

The QUARRELER

Rarr!

Frederick of Saxony	Louis X of France

The UNLUCKY

Arnulf III of Flanders	Henry III of Reuss

NOTHING TO SEA HERE...

We know more about the surface of the Moon than we do about the deepest part of the ocean.

Number of people who've been in space[*]

534

Number of people who've climbed Everest

over

3,000

Number of people who've been to the bottom of the ocean[**]   **3**

Don Walsh and Jacques Piccard made their journey in 1960. It took them 5 hours to reach the ocean bed and 3 hours and 15 minutes to get back.

The deepest part of the sea is called the Mariana Trench. Three people who have traveled there are Don Walsh, Jacques Piccard, and James Cameron—director of the film *Titanic*.

[*] From 1961 to 2013   [**] The Mariana Trench

6 inches

25¢ quarter

FUN WITH SIZE

Everything on these pages is exactly the same size as it is in real life.*

A dwarf lantern shark—the world's smallest shark

A bumblebee bat—the world's smallest mammal

*Except for the baby kangaroo. All of the other animals here are adults—their babies are even sma[ller]

Miracle Milly, the world's smallest living dog

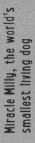
The world's smallest color TV screen. It was created in 2002.

The world's smallest book—created in Japan, you also received a magnifying glass so you could read it.

Thiomargarita namibiensis—the largest bacteria in the world.

Smallest unicycle wheel—Peter Rosendahl rode this unicycle 16 feet in 2011.

The smallest dinosaur footprint—The exact species of dinosaur that made the print is not known.

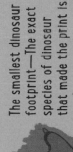

A baby kangaroo—The tiny joey crawls up its mother's belly and into her pouch, where it stays for 9 months.

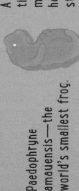

Paedophryne amauensis—the world's smallest frog.

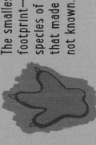

SEE YOU IN 3 DAYS...

This is how far you could travel in **3 days** at different times in history on different types of transport.

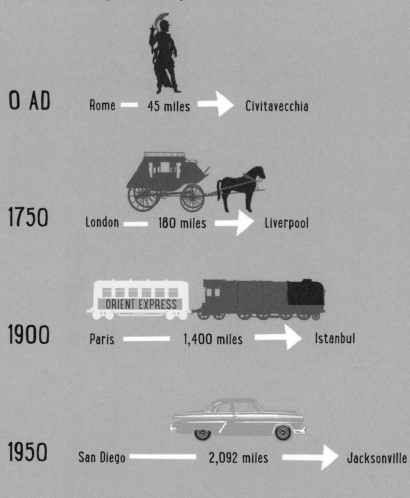

0 AD   Rome ———— 45 miles ➡ Civitavecchia

1750   London ———— 180 miles ➡ Liverpool

1900   Paris ———— 1,400 miles ➡ Istanbul

1950   San Diego ———— 2,092 miles ➡ Jacksonville

2000   Earth ————

238,855 miles

THE RED PLANET

A trip to Mars would take us between 5 and 9 months. That's roughly how long it would have taken a Roman army to march from Rome to London.

The Moon

OIL

The oil that we pump out of the ground is used—most famously—as fuel for our cars. But there are also hundreds of other things—from clothes to medicine—that wouldn't exist without this incredible substance. Here are a few of them...

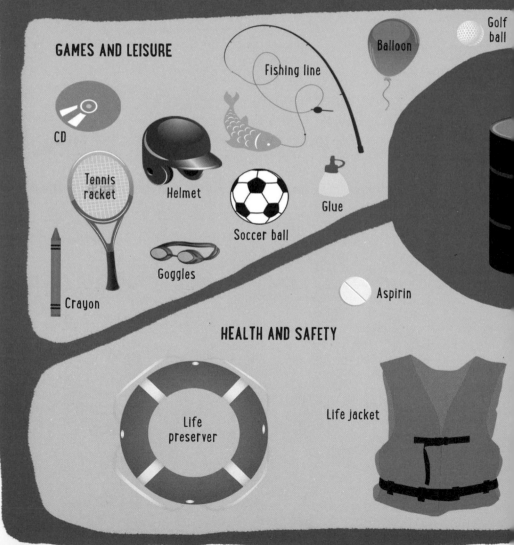

GAMES AND LEISURE

Balloon

Golf ball

Fishing line

CD

Tennis racket

Helmet

Soccer ball

Glue

Goggles

Crayon

Aspirin

HEALTH AND SAFETY

Life preserver

Life jacket

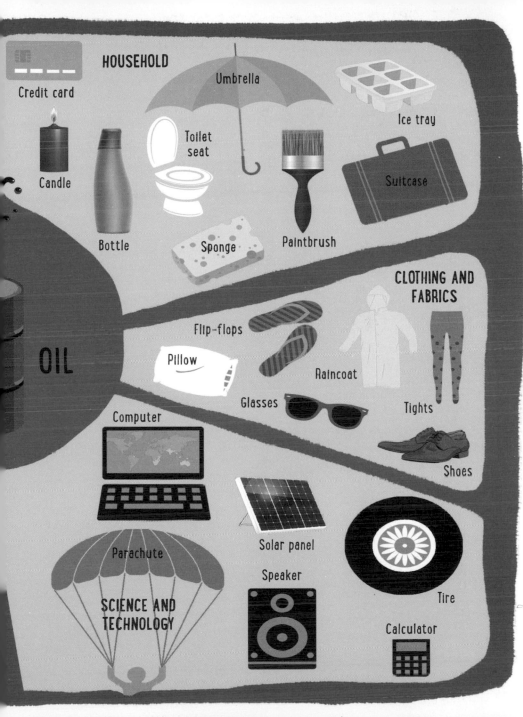

TOTALLY CRUSHED

Meet Albert the Alien. He comes from the Planet Sparg—where atmospheric pressure is 15,000 psi (pounds per square inch). So nothing on Earth can possibly crush him. Can it?

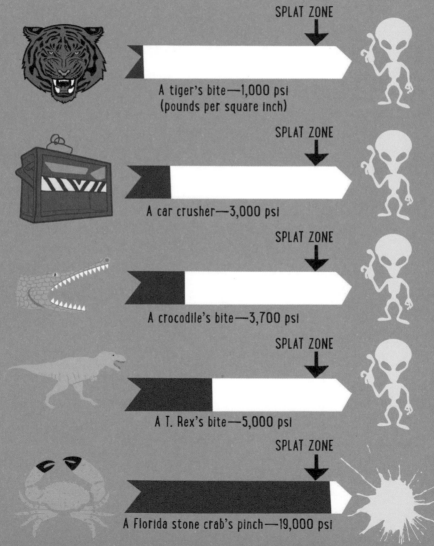

SPLAT ZONE

A tiger's bite—1,000 psi
(pounds per square inch)

SPLAT ZONE

A car crusher—3,000 psi

SPLAT ZONE

A crocodile's bite—3,700 psi

SPLAT ZONE

A T. Rex's bite—5,000 psi

SPLAT ZONE

A Florida stone crab's pinch—19,000 psi

SNOWFALL*

In 2011, Tomas Bergemalm reportedly broke the record for the highest free-fall cliff jump. In other words, he skied off a cliff without a parachute, relying on the snow to cushion his fall.

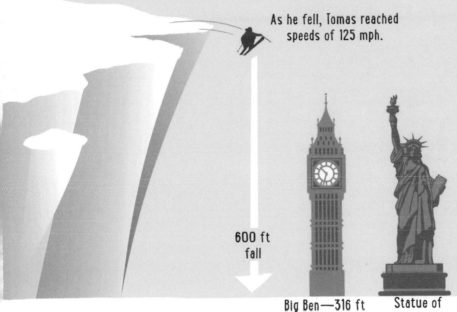

As he fell, Tomas reached speeds of 125 mph.

600 ft fall

Big Ben—316 ft

Statue of Liberty—305 ft

When Jamie Pierre performed a 255-ft free-fall jump in 2006, his landing made a 9 ft—wide crater.

He was completely unharmed by the jump, although he ended up with a cut lip from a shovel when his friends dug him out of the hole.

*These are world records and should never be attempted.

SEE YOU ONLINE

In just over a decade, the whole world has gotten used to living online.

Average Google searches per day

5.9 billion

60 million

2000

2013

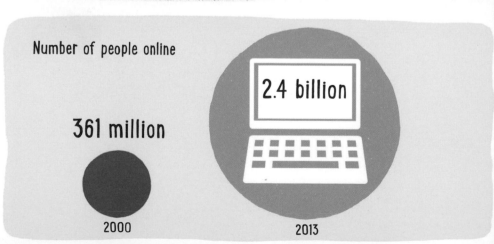

Number of people online

2.4 billion

361 million

2000

2013

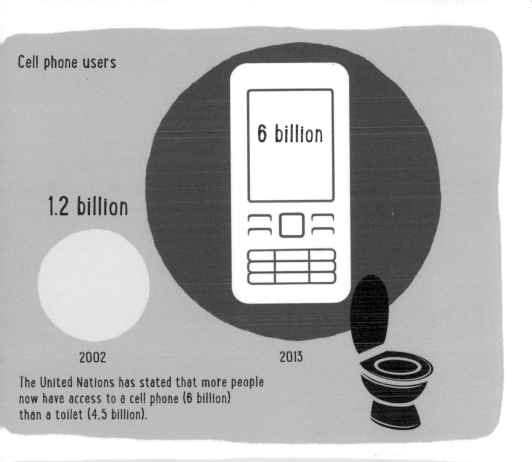

Cell phone users

6 billion

1.2 billion

2002   2013

The United Nations has stated that more people now have access to a cell phone (6 billion) than a toilet (4.5 billion).

Number of websites

1	130	100,000	162 million	670 million
1990	1993	1996	2008	2013

In 1990, there was just one website: info.cern.ch. It was set up by the inventor of the World Wide Web, Tim Berners-Lee. The website still exists.

SUPERBUGS

Insects and arthropods are creepy enough now, but in prehistoric times, they were even bigger and even "badder"!

Giant dragonfly
(Meganeura)
26 inches (in.) wingspan

Giant flea
At .9 in. long, this was 10 times the size
of modern fleas. It probably lived off pterosaur blood.

LAND

Giant scorpion
(Pulmonoscorpius)
28 in. long

Giant ant (Titanomyrma)
The queen of this species was 2 in. long.
That's almost twice as big as any ant living today.

Giant centipede (Arthropleura)
almost 9 ft

Giant flying extinct mothlike thin
(Mazothairos)
22 in. wingspan

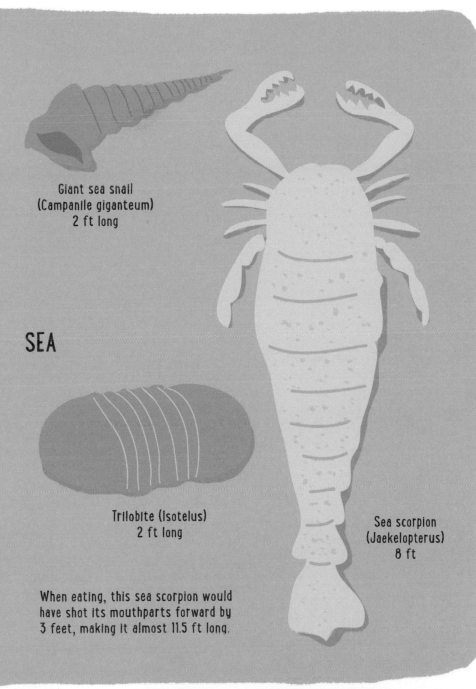

Giant sea snail
(Campanile giganteum)
2 ft long

SEA

Trilobite (Isotelus)
2 ft long

Sea scorpion
(Jaekelopterus)
8 ft

When eating, this sea scorpion would
have shot its mouthparts forward by
3 feet, making it almost 11.5 ft long.

SOURCES

This book would not have been possible without a wide range of other books, not to mention magazines, websites, tweets, and TV shows.
Here are some of the best.

BRILLIANT BOOKS:
Knowledge Encyclopedia (Dorling Kindersley, 2013)
Guinness World Records (Guinness World Records, 2013)
Children's Encyclopaedia of Animals (Dorling Kindersley, 2009)
The Natural World by Jon Richards and Ed Simkins (Owlkids, 2012)
Ripley's Believe It or Not 2014 by Ripley Publishing (Random House, 2013)
5000 Awesome Facts (About Everything) (National Geographic, 2012)
That's Gross! by Crispin Boyer (National Geographic, 2012)
Top 10 of Everything by Caroline Ash and Alexander Ash (Hamlyn, 2011)
The Big Book of Knowledge (Parragon, 2010)
How It Works Book of Junior Science (Imagine Publishing, 2013)
1227 QI Facts to Blow Your Socks Off—Kindle Edition by John Lloyd and John Mitchinson
    (Faber and Faber, 2012).
1339 QI Facts to Make Your Jaw Drop—Kindle Edition by John Lloyd and John Mitchinson (Faber and Faber, 2013)
    Plus the *QI* TV show and the QI Elves on Twitter
Boys' Miscellany by Martin Oliver (Buster Books, 2012)
Bumbelievable: The Bumper Book of Facts (Macmillan, 2013)
The How It Works Book of Amazing Answers to Curious Questions—Kindle Edition (Imagine Publishing, 2011)
Hmm...I Did Not Know That by A.P. Holiday—Kindle Edition (Haymaker, 2011)
Awesome Facts (Igloo, 2009)
You Won't Believe It But...(Igloo, 2010)

WONDERFUL WEBSITES:
www.britannica.com
http://kids.britannica.com
www.guinnessworldrecords.com
www.nationalgeographic.com
http://qi.com
http://uber-facts.com
www.newscientist.com
www.nasa.gov
www.lookandlearn.com
www.technologyreview.com
Newspaper websites: *Guardian, Independent, Huffington Post, Telegraph,* and *Daily Mail*
www.bbc.co.uk/news
www.theguardian.com
www.independent.co.uk
www.huffingtonpost.co.uk
www.telegraph.co.uk
www.dailymail.co.uk
And, of course, Google